I'll Be Glad to
Give a Devotion

I'll Be Glad to

Give a Devotion

Amy Bolding

BAKER BOOK HOUSE
Grand Rapids, Michigan

ISBN: 0-8010-0709-7

First printing, December 1977
Second printing, September 1978
Third printing, November 1979
Fourth printing, October 1980
Fifth printing, June 1981
Sixth printing, September 1982
Seventh printing, October 1983
Eighth printing, March 1985
Ninth printing, May 1986

PHOTOLITHOPRINTED BY CUSHING - MALLOY, INC.
ANN ARBOR, MICHIGAN, UNITED STATES OF AMERICA

CONTENTS

1

Wonderful! Wonderful!

There be three things which are too wonderful for me, yea, four which I know not: the way of an eagle in the air; the way of a serpent upon a rock; the way of a ship in the midst of the sea; and the way of a man with a maid.—Prov. 30:18, 19

How often we exclaim, "Isn't that wonderful!" Yet we go for days without thinking of the most wonderful thing in our lives—the gift of salvation from God.

After a long, cold winter spring sometimes comes suddenly. We look at fruit trees blooming or bulbs sending up green shoots and exclaim, "Isn't it a wonderful day!"

One year ago I was in a hospital having a serious operation for two malignancies. My heart was filled with fear and uneasiness. There were days of tests, days of suffering, days of getting well, and finally, the trip home. There is never a place as beautiful and warm as that special place we call home.

As the writer of Proverbs expressed, there are many things too great for us to understand. Therefore, we just accept them in the joy and knowledge that our heavenly Father has prepared them for us.

Life for all of us could be compared in many ways to a trip to the hospital. To live is to have some problems, some sorrows, some hard times, and some good times. Yet we keep living and remember in the back of our minds that the day will come when we will go to the home prepared for us by our Father.

I could not leave the hospital until medication and surgery had eliminated all the malignancy in my body.

When the doctor started talking about allowing me to go home in two days, my husband began to get things ready. He gave away the flowers that were filling the hospital room, he packed up books and magazines, then kept checking to see if he had forgotten anything.

Each day of our lives we know we are a little nearer the day we will go home. Are we checking to see if we have left something needful undone? Are we praying for grace and fortitude in daily trials? We cannot even think of an eternal home until our lives have been cleansed by the blood of Jesus Christ who died to make atonement for our sins.

When I returned home from the hospital, I didn't notice any of the things left out of place or the three weeks accumulation of dust; I only felt the joy and security of home.

Try this little exercise and see if your days are not happier and more peaceful. Get out of bed in the morning and look out the window. Name quickly the pleasant things you see. There might be a bird, a new flower or a small child; just train your eyes and heart to see the marvels of our world. We see and hear of miracles every day and sometimes we realize the greatness of God's love in making them come to pass. Other times we just ignore them.

After I arrived home from the hospital I was eager to write and call my loved ones to tell them the good news. Anything wonderful should be shared. Each day we should be enthusiastic about sharing our testimony with others.

We live in an exciting age. God has blessed America above all nations. The twentieth century has been a time of marvels. If I had told my grandmother when I was a small child that I would someday fly across the ocean, she would have scolded me and said I had a wild imagination, yet now it is a common trip for many people.

This is also a day of wonder concerning money. A penny was worth more when we stood before a candy counter in 1920. Now a dime will buy only a small piece. But still America is a wealthy nation. No one should go hungry in America.

I gave a little neighbor boy three pieces of chewing gum—one for himself, one each for his mother and father. In a few moments I looked at him and saw that he had all three pieces in his mouth. Will we be like the boy and take the wonders of God's love and keep them all?

Joy! Joy!

My life is filled with joy;
    I'm singing on my way;
The Lord has saved my soul
    And walks with me today.

There's hope within my heart,
    And sunshine is my lot;
Though storms rage overhead,
    My way they darken not.

My Lord and Savior makes
    My way so sweet to me
With His assurance that
    His love has set me free.

My sin He has forgiven;
    I'm not condemned, you see,
And now I have the joy
    Salvation brought to me.

J.T. Bolding

2

Power Failure

And the Spirit of the Lord will come upon thee, and thou shalt prophesy with them, and shalt be turned into another man. And let it be, when these signs are come unto thee, that thou do as occasion serve thee; for God is with thee.—I Sam. 10:6, 7.

When a transformer went out during an electrical storm, we were suddenly without many appliances that we take for granted and forget to count as blessings. The electric clocks stopped. The refrigerator and freezer stopped and frozen food started to thaw. We couldn't cook with our electric stove and there was no heat as the fan on the furnace wouldn't blow. Man's electrical power can fail but God's power can never fail. What if He suddenly withdrew His love and power from our lives! Who would heal the sick? Who would comfort the broken-hearted? Who would protect us from the evil of Satan? Who would guide us in our major decisions?

We go through each day enjoying good health, success in business, nice homes and friends. Then we have reverses: our health falters, our business fails, or our friends forget about us. Should we grow bitter?

We still have the same great power of God to help us. When

our electricity went off, servicemen were soon at the place of trouble to repair the transformer.

We must remember in troublesome times that the source of our strength and power is just as great as ever. We fail when we neglect to call upon that power and we grow bitter as we turn away from God's help.

It is harmful to have a power failure for just a few moments, but foolish for a Christian to turn away for long periods of time saying, "I have been hurt. God has neglected me and I will not worship Him again."

Two small girls were looking up at the sky on a warm spring day. Beautiful clouds were moving and making different types of designs.

"Who is holding those clouds up?" one girl asked.

"Why God, of course!" her companion said.

"Well, I wish I could meet Him; He is so strong," the other remarked.

When the power seems gone from your life do you wish you knew the One strong enough to hold up your burdens and give you rest?

Scripture says, "God is with thee." God has a purpose in all things. We do foolish things at times and blame them on God, yet He knows the choices we should make when we fail to ask Him.

To always be able to call on the power of God for help, we must first give Him our heart. If our heart belongs to God we are His child. A parent longs to see his child successful and happy. Would our heavenly Father be any less kind than an earthly parent?

God asks for our hearts because He owns all other things. But we are free agents and can withold our hearts from Him. Like the little girl looking at the clouds, we should want to know the One who is the source of all power.

After we have given our hearts to God, we need a powerline that is always in good repair. That powerline is prayer and Bible study—two simple things, yet they keep us strong and able to meet life.

There are forces in the world that try to break our powerline. Sin will burden it down until there is a break in communication. Uncertainty about life will make a wreck of a Christian. Fear, selfishness, greed, guilt, and modern idol worship will destroy our powerline. When we feel these worldly things gripping our lives, we must put them behind us. We must meet the One who holds up the clouds and ask Him to destroy the evil in our lives.

The psalmist wrote, "Cast thy burden upon the Lord, and he shall sustain thee: he shall never suffer the righteous to be moved" (Ps. 55:22).

How wonderful it was when our electrical power came back on that day. We cooked some good food, warmed up the house, and ran the carpet sweeper. It was a joy to have power again.

When you feel there has been a power failure in your life, turn back to the source of all power. How happy you will be. You will try to help others and you will seek to give rather than receive. Worldly things will be put in their place and God will be exalted.

An Example

It is not ours so much to see the future dim,
   As to finish well the task now close at hand;
Ours not so much to prophesy in praises prim,
   As to be found where God wants us to stand.

We are not duty bound our wisdom to reveal,
   Nor brag of all the things we have achieved;
But we should always seek some human hurts to heal
   And prove that God's own Word we have believed.

It's not required of us, that we impress our friends,
   And less, that we proclaim to them we're great;
But oh, how fine, if our example always tends
   To better them, if us they imitate.

J.T. Bolding

3

What Fragrance Do You Leave?

While the king sitteth at his table, my spikenard sendeth forth the smell thereof.—Song of Sol. 1:12

Having lived in western Texas for many years, where dust and wind often take away the sense of smell, I have grown used to not smelling.

Often people come in before mealtime and say, "Something sure smells good!" But I smell none of the aromas.

For a year I was ill, first with a broken ankle, then with an operation for the removal of two malignant tumors. Friends brought me flowers, bottles of hand lotion, bath powder and other gifts. Our house was full of things that smelled good, but I could not smell them.

One day a friend came by to take me to a meeting. I had put on scented hand lotion.

"My, you smell so nice today," she complimented me.

Suddenly a thought struck me: Christians should leave a sweet fragrance wherever they go. They should not just leave the fragrance of some earthly perfume, but a spirit of heavenly things.

The Scripture says, "While the king sitteth at his table, my spikenard sendeth forth the smell thereof."

As the sweet smell was in the room while the king was at the table, we should strive to leave a sweet feeling wherever we go.

At a meeting one night I sat in astonishment as a lady I had previously admired gossiped and said ugly things about another member of the class who was absent.

When the gossiper arose to leave early, I wanted to open the doors and windows to let the bad odor of gossip out.

Lately I have been teaching a Sunday school class for a teacher who is waiting for an operation on her eyes. She was able to attend a few Sundays when friends brought her. After class one of the members said, "She is such a great Christian that it is wonderful just to have her in the room."

Is it asking too much, if we say we are followers of Christ, to leave a sweet fragrance of love and kindness wherever we go?

In Genesis 8:21 we read, "And the Lord smelled a sweet savour; and the Lord said in his heart, I will not again curse the ground any more for man's sake. . . ." The Lord made this statement after Noah came out of the ark and offered a sacrifice unto the Lord. Today the Lord must smell a sweet savor when we attend worship services and offer Him our love and adoration.

My husband bought a used car. It was clean and had low mileage. I was pleased with it.

"Well," he told me a few days later, "the previous owner smoked and no amount of fresh air seems to get the smell out."

"Oh, I have some room freshener in the kitchen, maybe that will help it," I said.

"I don't believe an artificial freshener will smell much better than the smoke," he said. He could not be persuaded to use the artificial freshener.

Sometimes people want to leave a fragrance of good will and Christianity, but they do not really have Christ in their hearts. They may think they leave a sweet fragrance wherever they go without having a real born-again heart, but like the room freshener, it is artificial.

Fragrance

Some people, when they pass, will leave
    A rancid pipe's most acrid smell,
While some leave fumes of alcohol,
    And some, the awful breath of hell.

Sometimes a lovely girl may pass
    And such a charming fragrance trails;
But then sometimes a vicious guy
    With attitude as hard as nails.

Sometimes a personality,
    So very strong and good and kind,
Will pass along and touch one's life
    And leave a heavenly joy behind.

God gives life fragrance, fresh and clean,
    That stands close scrutiny and still
Is unafraid, for such well knows
    He walks in God's own holy will.

J.T. Bolding

4

Crumbs

And I was afraid, and went and hid thy talent in the earth: lo, there thou hast that is thine.—Matt. 25:25

When I was a child my mother often made bread pudding seasoned with nutmeg and cinnamon from leftover biscuits. Some people called bread pudding a poor folks' dessert. To a family of hungry children the pudding was a special treat.

What if my mother had thrown away the leftover bread? We could not have afforded cake or pie except on Sunday, so we would have longed for sweets the rest of the week.

At times we feel our talents are as just a few crumbs compared to the brilliant things we see other people doing.

We often refuse to make a visit or give a devotion because we feel others have more talent. Yet the word you had to say, or the experience you had to give, may have been just the inspiration someone needed.

Cold biscuits touched with my mother's magic hand were a real treat. Your talents, even if they are small, touched with God's glory, can bless others.

A friend of mine, looking for something useful to do, found an orphanage where she could visit the children. She was allowed to visit once a week to take the smaller children for nature walks.

That wasn't much of a task, yet it was what she knew how to do.

As they walked outside, my friend would point out flowers, bugs, and other types of growing things. A six-year-old named Tom always walked as close to her as possible. She would hold his hand or put her arm across his shoulder.

One day when the time came for her to go to the orphanage for her nature walk, she decided to stop going. But the face of that little boy came to her. She thought, "I am the only person who ever touches that child in a loving way."

She grabbed her hat and hurried to the orphanage. Tom was leaning against the gate watching for her. As they walked together to gather the other children, Tom asked her, "Are you Jesus' sister?"

"No, dear, I am just a woman who loves children," she answered.

"Well, I believe Jesus knows you," the child said simply.

In the sight of some adults, my friend was serving in a small way, but to a small boy she brought light and joy.

Someone needs your talent no matter how great or how small.

In our Scripture lesson we read about three men with talents. All received their talents from their master. One had five talents, one had two, and one had one. One man buried his talent. It therefore, could not grow and be useful. God was angry with him. His talent was taken away and he was punished.

So it is in life, some have more talents entrusted to them than others, yet all the talents are made in such a way that they will multiply if given the chance.

A certain fable tells of a time in winter when all the flowers and trees sleep except for the pansy. The pansy has a bright, gay face, even in the worst weather. A gardener stopped and said to the pansy, "Why are you so cheerful and bright while the others rest?"

"You planted me here, so I made up my mind to be the best, little flower I could," the pansy said.

If the pansy had said, "I want to be like the rose; I will not bloom and be so small," there would have been no bright, cheerful spot in the garden during the winter.

God gave each person something to do and a place to be useful. When you refuse to use the talent you have, some place is left bare and someone goes in need of your special gift. If your talents seem like crumbs from the table, determine to gather them up and make something useful of them.

A friend of mine has a sister confined to a wheel chair. Sometimes my friend takes a day off and takes her sister to shop in a mall. It is work to push her chair around, but it gives her sister much joy.

Many blind persons long to hear something read from a magazine or book. It only takes "crumbs" of time for the sighted one but is valuable to the blind.

If you think you have no talent, look around you and see if there is a person or a cause you can spare a few crumbs of time for.

During the forty-eight years of my husband's ministry, we were entertained in many lovely homes and were served many delicious meals. Now that he is retired, we have figured out a way to repay a few crumbs to our friends.

Western Texas is dry and lakes are scarce although there are a few small ones. We bought a small cabin about fifteen miles away from town on a lake. We often invite friends out for a meal and a ride in our sailboat.

Our furniture is not fine; a cabin is for fun, not show. My cooking doesn't have to be great; red beans and cornbread taste like a feast when you have walked along a lake shore and breathed fresh air.

You also probably have many crumbs of talent you are not using because you haven't thought about how happy they would make someone.

Do you drive a car? Many older people can't drive and would be happy to go riding. During the last years of my mother's life she liked us to take her driving around town. She had lived in the same town in Oklahoma for about forty years and could tell us about each school and church we passed. We gave just a little of our time, but she received a lot of joy.

Sometimes young people have a hard time communicating with older people, and thus neglect to visit them. Just because someone is old doesn't mean they should be forgotten.

In the Scripture, the master gave each servant at least one talent. Each was expected to multiply that talent. We often say, "I would enjoy teaching a Sunday school class or singing in the choir if I had time." Whatever your talent, use it now for it may be taken away if you bury it.

Your Plan

God has a plan for everyone
   And He has a plan for you;
He'll guide your life 'till its day is done,
   And will always see you through.

God has a goal for you to reach,
   And a life that He wants you to live;
He has a child for you to teach,
   And there's help that you need to give.

God has a star to light your way
   As He guides in the path He wills;
He'll give you strength for every day,
   As your heart with His love He fills.

J.T. Bolding

5

Bundle of Sticks

*Take therefore no thought for the morrow: for the morrow shall
take thought for the things of itself. Sufficient unto the day is the
evil thereof.—Matt. 6:34*

A few years ago a friend had a new house built. He wanted to
save all the lumber scraps to use in his new fireplace, so each afternoon when he finished work on his job, he hurried to the site
of the new house to gather all the bits and pieces of lumber that
he could find.

That plan was fine when the house was just being started, but
as the walls went up, there were more and more sticks and he
could not carry them all.

Finally the contractor spoke to him. "Why wear yourself out
carrying those scraps, I will pile them over to one side and you
can get them when the house is finished," he said.

The owner of the new home wondered why he had not asked
the builder to care for the scraps in the first place instead of taking a few at a time.

We are often like this man. We try to carry yesterday's prob-
lems, today's problems and tomorrow's problems all at one time.
Our load would be much lighter if we could only trust the Master
Builder to care for our sticks.

In I Kings 17:12-13 we read the story of a poor widow gathering sticks to cook her last meal. She had gathered two sticks for a small fire when God's prophet, Elijah, came by and brought her a blessing. Elijah asked the widow for part of her food. She could have refused as there was little food left, but she believed his promise that God would supply plenty of meal to meet her future needs.

We miss many blessings because we fail to trust our bundle of sticks to the care of the Builder.

Due to a siege of illness, I felt just about like the poor widow. The world seemed blue and hopeless. But then my phone rang. A high school boy was calling to ask for an interview. An hour later when he was seated in our living room, my attitude changed. Here was a boy with ambition to write great books who needed my encouragement. I am sure I failed to tell him any technical secrets because I just write from my heart, but he needed me to share my love for writing with him. He helped me, because he needed me. I helped him, because I knew the world was waiting for something fresh and new.

We often fail to see the beauty of today because we are worrying about the cold spell predicted for tomorrow. That is what Jesus meant when He said, "Take therefore no thought for the morrow: for the morrow shall take thought for the things of itself. Sufficient unto the day is the evil thereof."

My oldest daughter is the mother of five children. As the children were growing up, she often wondered how she and her husband could send five children to college. When the day came for the oldest girl to go away to school, the whole family was interested in her. She received a scholarship and also found a job to ease the family's financial burden.

That bundle of sticks was carried so joyously and so easily, my daughter forgot how she had worried. In two more years their next child was ready to attend the same college, then one year later their twin boys started. All four attended college at the same time.

God was good to open up the way as things were needed. The

two oldest have graduated and have good jobs and husbands, the twins will finish in another year. The youngest child is just getting ready for junior high.

Of course there were many anxious moments. There were times when tuition and books seemed almost too much to afford, but one at a time, their problems were handled and needs met.

A small child in a Sunday school class was asked, "Does your daddy read the Bible at home?"

"No," the child said "but he reads it at church."

Many of us are like the child's father. We never think to talk our problems over with the Lord until Sunday when we could be having comfort and strength all week. We all seem to seek a lighter burden. Yet look around; some of the happiest people you know have large burdens to carry.

Gather up your little sticks of burdens, and your larger ones as well. Then place them all at the feet of the Lord and ask Him to care for them and feel your burden lighten.

God's Care

Though the day is cold and dreary
When the sun neglects to shine,
And my bones grow sore and weary,
I have not a need to pine.
And my heart within grows cheery;
On God's goodies I can dine;
Oft my eyes with tears grow bleary
For I know, God's best is mine.

J.T. Bolding

6

Touch the Hem of His Garment

And when the men of that place had knowledge of him, they sent out into all that country round about, and brought unto him all that were diseased; And besought him that they might only touch the hem of his garment: and as many as touched were made perfectly whole.—Matt. 14:35, 36

There come times in life when we feel helpless and afraid and need the strength of another human to lean on. I needed such strength one Christmas Eve when I was alone in the house and my sister called to tell me our mother had just died.

My husband was in his workshop finishing some gifts he had made for the grandchildren. As I didn't want to rush out to tell him until I had gotten over the shock, I waited.

Placing my head on the table by the phone, I leaned on the One who has the strength for all problems. I thanked Him for letting Mother slip away quietly without a lot of suffering. I thanked Him for letting her step into the world where my father and two baby brothers waited. What a Christmas they would have!

After a few moments with the One who had given me strength since childhood, I could break the news to my husband. Like the people in Scripture I had touched the hem of His garment and received strength.

It is important that we are selective in choosing good friends. I knew a girl in school who felt left out of social affairs. Her mother was a hard-working widow who could not afford any luxuries for her daughter.

In desperate loneliness the daughter turned to a girl of rough character for companionship.

One evening her mother asked, "Do you know Kay Bridges?"

"Yes, we are pretty good friends," the girl answered.

"Please don't be unkind," her mother said, "but drop your friendship with her." The mother explained, "One of my customers told me the police have been asking questions about Kay. They suspect she might be in serious trouble."

"Mother, I have to have someone for a friend."

"If you study hard and keep yourself pure and sweet, some nice friends will come," the mother told her.

Because she took more time to study and found a part-time job, Lea was asked to join an honor society. There she "touched the hem" of some of the best minds in school. Soon she was respected and had plenty of friends.

Americans are notorious hero-worshipers. We honor and admire athletes, inventors, and other heroes. We are all influenced by people we associate with. The Bible has many stories of great leaders. Hebrews 12:2, says, "Looking unto Jesus, the author and finisher of our faith. . . ." It is God's plan that we look to the greatest One of all time.

A ball player named Ron was resentful because the coach had announced a student day at the start of practice season.

The football field was to be open and the players were to be on hand to greet all the visitors, give them autographs, and let them feel the new artificial turf.

"We are just wasting our time," Ron complained. "Let them wait until the games start and buy their tickets."

When the students started coming, the players were swamped with boys handing up pens and note pads.

Suddenly Ron broke away and ran toward the gate. Everyone looked to see what had happened.

Out on the edge of the field stood a woman behind a wheel chair. In the chair sat a small boy, twisted and crippled. Ron scooped the child up in his arms and took him over to the crowd.

"Everyone give my friend an autograph," he commanded. The child laughed with glee, enjoying himself more than any of the lively children milling about.

After Ron took the child back to his mother and the players were ready to start a game, Ron said to his best buddy, "It just wasn't fair for a little kid like that not to get in on the fun."

"I'll never complain about a hard workout after seeing that poor kid," his friend replied.

What are we in pursuit of as we touch the hem of many garments during the days of our lives? Too many lives are being spent in pursuit of the wrong things, unworthy things.

The people who came to touch the hem of Christ's garment were in search of the necessary things—health, food, and knowledge of a kingdom to come.

Between People, Bridges

Everybody builds some bridges
  Which are meant to help or bless;
Some cross rivers or join ridges
  To relieve someone's distress.

Bridges take on many natures
  And appear in lots of forms,
Bearing varied nomenclatures
  As they quiet problem storms.

Clasped or waving or extended,
  Hands may bridge some chasms wide,
Helping broken ties he mended
  As dear folk walk side by side.

Books, ideas, words and glances
  Help good hearts search for a way,
As kind look and thought advances,
  Bridging people-gaps each day.

J.T. Bolding

7

Expired Coupons

Whereas ye know not what shall be on the morrow. For what is your life? It is even a vapour, that appeareth for a time, and then vanisheth away.—James 4:14

One evening my husband noticed some coupons in the afternoon paper.

"You should cut out all these coupons; you can save a lot on your groceries tomorrow," he said. "Don't forget to cut them out."

I dutifully found my scissors and cut out coupons for discounts on sugar, shortening, frozen dinners and a few other smaller items.

Friends came to visit the next day, and I forgot about the grocery store. Two days later I went, coupons in hand, to buy my groceries. Imagine how deflated I felt when I arrived at the checkout counter and the clerk told me my coupons had all expired. I had just waited a few days too long.

Many people have the same attitude about life. They intend to serve the Lord—later. They really think it is the thing to do, but company comes in.

Desire is that company—desire for making money, desire for having fun and good times, or desire for pleasurable things that are not necessarily bad, but take so much of our time and money that they keep us from the best.

The first year I was married, I really wanted to have a part in the little country church near us. We went most of the time, but sometimes we didn't make an effort.

One Sunday I was given a part in the evening program. That was a big deal for an eighteen-year-old girl and I wanted to do a good job. I assured the lady in charge that I would be there on time.

The afternoon was so beautiful, that it seemed the thing for us to do was to ride around the countryside, then go to church. Late in the afternoon we noticed time running out, so we were anxious to get to the church.

"We will open this gate and go across the pasture; it should save us several miles," my husband said as he got out to open the wire gate so I could drive through. After he was back in the car, he gave it all the speed it would take and we started zooming across the pasture.

"We can save miles and be there on time," he said.

Without realizing what was happening, we drove right into a mud hole. He spun the wheels, but nothing resulted. That old Model T didn't care whether we went to church or not.

"I see a faint light down there at that ranch house," my husband said. "You sit here and wait; I will get help."

Dark had already settled in and I thought of the cows we had seen as we were driving along and I started to cry, "I am afraid of the cows!"

"Stay in the car; they won't hurt you!" he said as he got out of the car. "What if you had to walk way down there for help?"

He was aggravated and slammed the door hard. The glass broke in hundreds of pieces.

Two silly children had let their coupons of time run out needlessly.

Much more foolish are the people who put off service for the Lord. The day comes when they seek someone to blame, as I blamed my husband. But each person is responsible for his own response to God. Blame company, loved ones, friends, or work, but nothing will keep your coupons of life from running out.

A woman I know never married. She had a good job and enjoyed giving things away. Her friends and loved ones told her to save money because her parents were dead and she had only herself to depend on.

"I want to enjoy now. I will save when I am old," she told them.

"Please don't spend so much on your friends; we would much rather see you build up some savings," her friends would say when she gave an expensive gift.

Then one day she became ill and had doctor bills to pay. Her car broke down at the same time and had to have expensive repairs. The woman had nothing to fall back on.

After that experience she realized her plight and started saving.

Life for each of us is short at best and we can't put off cashing our coupons for we do not know when they will expire.

Now

Why fret about tomorrow
   When you have this precious day?
Why fill it up with sorrow
   As you waste the hours away?

These moments are your treasure,
   And tomorrow may not come;
Let God's will be your pleasure,
   As you scatter joy to some.

Why fret about God's blessings,
   And complain they're not enough,
Or think it so distressing
   That you have so little stuff?

This day so soon will vanish,
   And the past you can't recall;
All fears you need to banish;
   Play the game! You have the ball!

                J.T. Bolding

8

The Sidetracks of Life

The slothful man roasteth not that which he took in hunting: but the substance of a diligent man is precious.—Prov. 12:27
And the things that thou hast heard of me among many witnesses, the same commit thou to faithful men, who shall be able to teach others also.—II Tim. 2:2

I have a friend named Jean who is always talking of the big things she is going to do. She will plan to paint a picture, but she never starts. She will set a time to make a visit but gets sidetracked by some other diversion.

Often her friends laugh about some committee unmet or some affair unattended, and say, "You know Jean; she probably got sidetracked."

Proverbs 12:27 pictures a man who has been hunting for food. He finds game and kills it. He is hungry, but when he returns home, he fails to cook the food. It is wasted.

During 1974 when food prices started getting higher and higher, many families planted gardens. One family gathered the food they raised and put it in a freezer. That winter their table was always full of home-grown vegetables.

Another family planted a garden. Their vegetables grew and

produced, but because they didn't like to work in the garden in hot weather, they let others come in and pick the vegetables.

That family decided they would pick and freeze their harvest when the weather got cooler. But the harvest season passed and they never felt that it was the right time to gather food.

Beans dried up on the vines and tomatoes rotted in the field. Needless to say, that family complained the loudest when cold winter came and their table was bare.

Sidetracks keep many young people from being a success in life. When something looks inviting down the road, they turn aside to investigate it.

A boxer was once asked how he made such a success out of his career.

"I followed the advice of my father," he said. "When I told him I was going to try for a boxing career, he looked at my strong body, patted me on the back, and told me, 'If you are going to fight, fight in Madison Square Garden, not in a back alley.' From that time on, I never let the alleys tempt me; I headed for Madison Square Garden."

To reach any goal is a struggle, yet it can be done if we avoid sidetracks. Life is not worth much if we avoid all the struggles.

What is the main track and what is a sidetrack?

The main track for any Christian is found in our second verse, "The things thou hast heard of me among many witnesses, the same commit thou to faithful men, who shall be able to teach others also."

We are to tell the story of Jesus and His love.

One rainy day when I was in the first grade, our teacher taught us how to make paper chains. She cut some magazines in strips and passed them out. Soon paste bottles were open and we were intent on making chains. Each wanted to make the longest. We forgot that the rain was coming down outside. We forgot all about not having a recess that day. We made chains.

One child thought it would be fun if we could make a chain long enough to reach from our desks to the teacher's desk. In an hour she looked like the hub of a maypole. To us those chains seemed exciting and beautiful. Our teacher complimented each one.

Jesus started a chain of Christian believers that has grown longer and longer over the two thousand years since his birth.

Faithful witnesses still make chains of love from the hearts of men to Jesus. He stands in the center like our dear teacher stood for us that winter day.

When one becomes a link in the chain of witnessing and love, he should immediately seek to win someone else.

A small boy who had worked making some kind of a contraption on wheels, asked a friend for a push.

"Which way do you want to go?" the friend asked.

"I don't care as long as it is forward," he answered.

No sidetrack appealed to that child; he wanted to go forward.

I know a young man who went through college, but was lazy about hunting for a job, therefore found no job, so started school again. When he finished his masters degree the family felt sure he would look for a job, but instead he asked for a trip to a foreign country.

Back from his trip the parents pressured him more to get a job. He had been on so many sidetracks, he forgot what he had gone to school for in the beginning.

The poor young man reminds me now of an old boxcar sitting on a sidetrack, useless, abandoned, and forgotten. He is spending what should be the most productive time of his life sidetracked at his mother's bountiful table.

As Christians we often get sidetracked and fail to go and give the message. Christians like the young man, often seek things that are in themselves good, but keep us from going forward to win the world for Christ.

Let Us All Sing

Let us all sing a sweet song of the love
  Of our Savior and Lord: Christ our king;
Let us all sing of His glory above
  Making voices with melody ring.

Let us each labor at the task He ordains
  And continually strive to please Him;
Let us all work with a will that sustains
  Though the cloud and the storm make hope dim.

Let us all give of our best every day,
  That the world may know Christ and be saved;
Let us share the good news as we stay
  Ever close to the One our hearts craved.

Let us all love as He taught us to do,
  And not merely the ones who love us,
But with concern in our hearts that is true
  To folks' needs, without making a fuss.

Let us all wait with our hearts full of joy
  For the certain return of the Lord;
Let us all work as His songs we employ,
  And live patiently in sweet accord.

                                        J.T. Bolding

9

I Had the Worries!

Lest my father leave caring for the asses, and take thought for us.—*I Sam. 9:5b*

Therefore take no thought, saying, What shall we eat? or, What shall we drink? or, Wherewithal shall we be clothed? . . . your heavenly Father knoweth that ye have need of all these things, but seek ye first the kingdom of God, . . . and all these things shall be added unto you.—*Matt. 6:31, 32b, 33*

A college boy was talking to me about trying to get into a certain honor society. He said "I have the worries."

The boy made the society, and his worries were forgotten.

Jesus knew there would be times when his followers would "have the worries." He did not want this to be true, so to encourage us He gave us Matthew 6:31-33.

Parents often grow uneasy when children are away from home and do not return when expected.

I heard a story on the news of a twelve-year-old boy who thought his dog was lost. He went into the woods to look for the dog, but in a few hours the dog had returned home and the boy was lost. Searchers did not find him for two days. The boy worried needlessly about his dog, but because he had worried, he caused great anxiety to parents and friends by becoming lost.

My neighbor across the street works hard all week, but on Sunday he looks forward to spending the afternoon reading the newspaper. One day when snow was deep on the porch the paperboy took pains to place the paper in the mail box.

My neighbor went to the door, looked on the porch, but saw no paper. He fretted and fumed and finally called the paperboy.

"Early this morning it was snowing hard, so I put your paper in the mailbox, out of the snow," the boy told him.

My neighbor had looked down rather than up for the paper, so he had the worries.

Our heavenly Father looks at our lives and sees the things we are fretting about all safe in their place waiting to be worked out in His time.

Many times we get the worries from judging people. Someone says or does something we do not understand so we get hurt or angry.

One night at church a friend of mine turned and walked away as I approached her. I was hurt and worried. What had I said or done to make her act in such a manner?

I worried for several days, wondering if I should call her. I decided against it as things sometimes sound different on the phone.

In a few days I went to a meeting and saw my friend all alone on the back seat. I sat down by her and asked, "Are you angry with me about something?"

"Oh, no," she said, "this has been such a hard week for me I am not myself."

Then I remembered that her husband had been ill and died a year ago that week. How ashamed I felt for not thinking of her sorrow and instead judging her as being unkind and cross.

To remind me of my worries and mistake I wrote:

> I will not judge,
> I will not judge,
> No matter what folks say.
> For if I judge,
> I might judge wrong,
> And take some joy away.

Having the worries gets to be a habit. We should try, when we feel the symptoms coming on, to stop and think of all the good things we have to be thankful for.

Of course there are crises in every life, sometimes many, and I would hate to cross over the seas of crises without Christ to guide me.

We often get so tied up in our problems that we feel we are living in a pressure cooker with the valve ready to pop any moment.

When we were young, my husband and I started planning how we would educate our three children. We often asked God to guide and help us, but we did not stop there. We tried to put away a little money each month for the days to come.

When the children were all educated and away from home we started thinking about a home to live in for our old age. Again, we had to diligently save.

God gives us salvation, a free gift of love; yet we must not stop there. We need to think of the day when we will meet him face to face. We want to hear him say, "Well done!"

We need to build up credit in our spiritual lives, so when a day of worries comes, we can draw on that credit.

Matthew 8:26 reads, "Why are ye fearful, O ye of little faith?"

Mark 4:40, reads, "Why are ye so fearful? how is it that ye have no faith?"

In the light of these verses, a Christian should never have the worries.

I will never forget the story a dear friend told me about her wedding. She was afraid if she asked her parents for permission to be married they would say no. So she and her sweetheart planned to run away. The boy's brother agreed to help them, by taking them to a small town in his car.

Ollie dressed in two of everything she had and then pinned her hat on.

The brother-in-law took the young couple to a minister in a small town across the state line.

"I'll have to put some clothes on," the minister called from inside the house.

"We don't care what you put on; just hurry," they shouted.

The door opened at last. The minister stood there with his coat and trousers over his pajamas with no shirt or tie on.

When the minister finished, the groom reached over and kissed the bride. He was so fervent that he caused her hat to fall off. Out rolled yards and yards of tatting. She had not been able to leave her dearest treasure at home, so she hid it in her hat.

Thirty-eight years later she showed me the tatting, still unfinished. She never found time to finish that work of art she had started as a sixteen-year-old girl.

We often worry and are fearful for treasures which really never find a useful purpose in our lives.

Use Me, Lord

If I have a talent, Lord,
    Whatever it may be,
Use that talent, Lord,
    To turn someone to Thee.

If I have ability, Lord,
    For some very special task,
Use that ability, Lord,
    To glorify Thee, I humbly ask.

If I have a special skill, Lord,
    Point it out to me;
Help me use that skill, Lord,
    In service unto Thee.

Many things You have given me, Lord:
    Health and home and loved ones, dear.
Help me to give them all to Thee, Lord,
    And to serve Thee year after year.

Lela Bristow Tadlock

10

Required Course

Moreover it is required in stewards, that a man be found faithful.—I Cor. 4:2

When I was in high school, we were required to take a foreign language class. Our school offered a choice of Spanish or Latin.

I am sure I made the wrong choice in selecting Spanish. To this day, I can speak only a few words of that musical language.

But once I had signed up for the course I was forced to be faithful in learning it for the next nine months.

What a drag. I was bored for those nine months and my teacher must have been equally bored, for she never inspired me to even want to speak Spanish.

How different it is when one commits his life to Christ and His kingdom! If we are truly committed we want to go out and tell the world. We want to see others sign up for the same course.

In life there are many required courses. Many courses we resent having to take, yet they are, in the long run, good for us.

Remember the story of Daniel and his friends. They were captives far from home, yet they stayed on the diet they had been taught to follow in their homeland. Even the king was pleased with their growth.

It seems hard for some adults, as well as youths, to follow the required course for good growth and health.

It is great to grow and be well physically, but is much greater to grow spiritually.

A man who had trusted Christ in childhood had never grown up spiritually into a working Christian. He attended church services if his family insisted, but he found no real joy in going.

A new pastor came to the church. He took the roll and started making a list of all the things he wanted accomplished around the church. With list in hand and great faith in God, the young man started out.

When he came to the immature Christian he said to him, "I want you to be at the church tonight to look over the plumbing. It will be your task to help me get it in good shape."

He appointed another man to check all the windows to see if some needed repair. On and on the young preacher went.

When the men arrived that evening they were surprised to find others there. After a word of prayer the young pastor turned them loose to complete their assignments.

Before long one of the men brought a friend with him. He said his friend knew more about plumbing than he did and if he required pay, he would pay him. That man was won to Christ by the pastor as he worked—not by sermons, but by kind words and Christian example.

Without realizing what was happening the men of that church became faithful workers; they enlisted and won others. The pastor led them in prayer growth, in financial growth, and in letting their lights shine.

When we have set our lives on a required course we must be faithful, enthusiastic, and prayerful. Sometimes it is hard to remain faithful, but we must remember that the faithful will receive rewards.

A fable tells of a king who placed a large stone on a road. All day people walked around the stone and complained about it. Late in the afternoon a boy woodcutter on his way home came to the rock.

"Some traveler might stumble on this rock and be hurt," he thought.

He tugged at the rock to move it from the road. Even though his arms hurt from swinging an axe all day, he moved the rock. Under the rock he found a bag of gold with a note on it.

The boy could not read, so he went to the king and asked him to read the note.

The king was very happy that he had found one subject who would work for others without seeking a big pay.

The king read, "take this gold and go to school, learn your lessons well, then come back and help me rule."

God sent His Son to earth for the purpose of providing redemption for our sins. What if Christ had not been faithful?

As Christians we have a duty; someone will suffer if we are not found faithful in witnessing, praying, and helping others.

Knowing what is right and doing what is right are two different things. When we are growing up our parents set a required course for us to follow. For instance, we must be home at a certain hour, eat certain food and rest a required time. If we fail to meet these requirements we are punished.

God has His required course for us to follow, too. If we follow God's requirements for a Christian life we will be happy and useful.

Two small boys were throwing a ball in the house. They knew their mother required them to play ball in the yard. The mother was busy in the kitchen, so they were sure they would get by with their play.

Suddenly the ball hit a lamp and broke it. The mother ran into the room.

"We didn't intend to hit it mother!" they exclaimed.

"You didn't have to intend to; you were so close you couldn't miss it," she said.

The boys were punished. They had to take money from their allowance for many weeks to replace the lamp.

The grandmother thought the punishment was too severe, but the mother said, "There are required courses in life, and they might just as well learn now that when we fail to meet those requirements we are punished," she said.

Another woman had a bad habit of going to an expensive store where she had a charge account to buy evening dresses. She would take a dress home, wear it to a party, then bring it back to the store to return it. After having dirty dresses returned several times, the clerk took the matter to the manager.

"We will post a sign that any merchandise which has been worn will not be taken back," he decided.

In a few days the lady came to get a dress. She selected a very expensive one and went gaily out the door.

Before she could return the dress a bill was sent from the store. Her husband opened the bill and saw the price of the dress.

"You know we can't afford such an expensive dress," he told her.

"Don't worry, I will take it back today," the wife assured him.

When the lady arrived at the store with the dress she was surprised to have the clerk refuse to take it. She threatened to cause all kinds of trouble if she could not return the dress.

The manager was called and he stood firm, "We have had several cleaning bills from your returning dresses," he said. "Our new policy will stand."

The woman was charged for the dress and her husband missed a business opportunity because he had to pay her bills.

The person who expects to get by without going the required way will eventually be discovered and punished. It takes courage to say no when asked to step aside from the required ways of law and right, but following the required course of honest living pays off in self-respect and clear conscience.

Life's Current

It's so easy to drift with the current each day,
   To avoid the distasteful or difficult way,
When a need calls upon us to do as we say,
   We ought to face facts and then do what we can.

When great sorrow and sadness around us we see,
   When there's heartache and illness from which we are free,
And a friend's overloaded I'm sure you'll agree,
   That we ought to face facts and then help what we can.

J.T. Bolding

11

We Can't Quit Now

He becometh poor that dealeth with a slack hand: but the hand of the diligent maketh rich.—Prov. 10:4

In 1970 the small city where I live was torn to pieces by a tornado. Twenty-six people were killed and many were injured. Several businesses were blown away or badly damaged.

One businessman lost almost his entire stock and the building was in shambles. After walking around and seeing the extent of his loss, he walked away.

What could he do? He was middle-aged, he had children in college, and his means of livelihood was gone.

As he came to the corner where he was accustomed to stopping for a shoe shine, he stopped and spoke to the shine boy.

The boy had a bright smile on his face. He had a shine cloth in his hand ready to go to work.

"I can't afford a shine today," the man sighed, "Look down there at my store."

"Well, you're gonna build it back up, aren't you?" the boy asked.

"I doubt it; I was only partially covered with insurance," the man answered.

"Do you think God is dead just because we had a storm?" the boy said as he waved the shine cloth around. "He will help you."

"Of course He is not dead!" the man said as his drooping shoulders squared. "Shine me up, son, I'll go see about borrowing some money."

Many people wondered what they should do during those troubled weeks following the storm. People from all over Texas sent help. The people who were not in the path of the storm helped those who were wiped out. A new sense of helpfulness and brotherhood prevailed.

Many fathers and mothers felt like giving up because their load was so heavy, but love for each other and duty to their children, kept them going.

Mrs. Dwight D. Eisenhower once said her favorite verse was Psalm 91:11, "For he shall give his angels charge over thee, to keep thee in all thy ways."

Imagine the many times in her life when her husband and son were away in war that she clung to God's promise to, keep us in all our ways.

Another famous personality, Mrs. J.C. Penney gave her favorite verse as Psalm 121:1, 2. "I will lift up mine eyes unto the hills, from whence cometh my help."

You might think of these two ladies and feel they had no cause to ever feel like quitting, yet their problems were as real to them as your problems are to you.

If we have our hearts and life anchored in the God of our salvation, when we feel we can't go on, we will go on, because our anchor will hold and we will receive new strength from above.

We are all going to meet times of discouragement. We must take those times as temporary and re-evaluate our blessings. We can't quit just because we planned a picnic and the sand blew that day.

Monty Brown was a boy who grew up quitting. When he was on the high school basketball team the coach failed to let him play one game. The next day Monty turned in his equipment.

When Monty secured a job he was doing very well until his girl friend said, "I don't think they appreciate you in that office." Then he started looking for another job. His life went on in such a manner until one day he came under the influence of a good counselor. He saw that a quitter never wins and a winner never quits.

Americans are, by nature, a hopeful people. We always talk about what we will accomplish in the future. That is fine, except we must realize that today is the future of yesterday.

Scripture says, "He becometh poor that dealeth with a slack hand."

We must not be slack about our work. Some people think so much of the goals set for tomorrow that they cannot enjoy the beauty of today.

Hubert Humphrey said, "I like to spend my time working for things that are to come, not looking back on disappointments."

Missionary parents in a foreign land were sending their son back to the United States for college. The father took the son aside and handed him the following note:

> You will be lonely,
> And you will be afraid,
> Sometimes.
> Both are an inescapable part of life.
> Keep on keeping on!

All people, whether at home or far away, feel like giving up at times. There is a strength that keeps us going against all odds. That strength comes from our faith in God and our deep abiding knowledge that He cares for us in spite of our faults and failures.

A doctor's wife I know is very often bothered with depression. She determined to overcome those spells by baking a cake for someone each time she felt depressed. One day she told me she baked three cakes before she could smile and be happy.

To make others happy is a great virtue, a gift from God, a blessing to the world. When life seems useless and you want to quit, look about and think of at least two people you know who are worse off than you are.

Proverbs 10:4 tells us to take hold of life with a firm hand and to be diligent about our work and affairs.

Take hold of yourself when tempted to quit a task. Every pastor and Sunday school teacher has felt that they just had to quit preaching or teaching at sometime during their service. But someone said an encouraging word and let them know they were needed, so they kept on keeping on.

Why do some old people live more active and happier lives than others? They have a positive attitude. They grow older, but they never get old. Every year of life to them is a bonus.

My Son

When the breaks have gone against you,
   Keep your courage up, my son.
When you're sure that you are beaten
   And you long to turn and run,
Lift your eyes and square your shoulders
   Till in you a victory's won.
Life goes on, and you go with it;
   Keep your courage up, my son.
When the day is dark and stormy,
   Keep your courage up, my son.
When you fail, or fall, or stumble,
   Or life's blows confuse and stun,
Raise your head and face the future;
   Let your work all be well done,
And resolve to please the Master;
   Keep your courage up, my son.

                  J.T. Bolding

12

A Man Needs a Toolchest

Then the word of the Lord came unto me, saying, Before I formed thee in the belly I knew thee; and before thou camest forth out of the womb I sanctified thee, and I ordained thee a prophet unto the nations.—Jer. 1:4, 5

From this Scripture we might deduce that God has a purpose for each person, even before they are born.

His purpose for Jeremiah was to be a prophet unto the nations.

If you admit to the above Scripture, then you must believe that God has a purpose for your life.

The question you face is, "Am I fulfilling my purpose and do I have the proper tools to use in fulfilling my purpose?"

My husband and I have been counseling a young man who started college two years ago with the firm conviction he would become a college math teacher.

For some reason, this year he has become uncertain about that goal. His grades are good, he has a good job, yet he is torn to pieces and can't get settled.

If he goes on in his present state of uncertainty he will not succeed at anything. He will have a toolchest filled with knowledge, yet no inspiration about what to build.

We have told him to pray for God's leadership. Perhaps God has not yet revealed his plan for him, but he must rest assured that God does have a plan for his life.

God does not plan for all his children to be made from one mold, for one task.

Our world would be dull if all men were ministers, and all women were housekeepers. God has many tasks and calls for many to serve in different ways.

I married when I was eighteen years old. My mother had never taught me to cook, so you can imagine some of the dishes I set before my new husband. My toolchest was completely empty as far as knowledge about cooking went. Breakfast food and milk kept us from starving until I learned.

We owe many debts to the people who are kind and help us grow up. If you look back at your life, you will find many little nuggets of knowledge you learned from some faithful person. That person used the tools he had to help another.

How I wish I could go back to the homes of all the good women in my husband's churches who taught me to cook. Most of them are in heaven now, so I know they are reaping rewards.

Let's pretend for a moment that we have been given a new toolbox of life. What should we put in it?

We need salvation and a firm trust in Jesus Christ. Then it follows as night follows day that we need the Golden Rule in our chest. Luke 6:31 says, "And as ye would that men should do to you, do ye also to them likewise."

There are many other tools listed in Scripture that we should also have.

From time to time we must examine our tools and see that they are in good working order. Sometimes we get in the habit of forgetting the other fellow and his needs.

There are also some tools we do not want in our toolbox.

Once at a meeting, I saw a woman trying to put down one of the other guests. Something was mentioned about stamps given with purchases at the grocery store. No one present knew where the stamps went when food was purchased for use at the church or for people in need.

One of the women present was on the committee that purchased food for the poor. She mentioned that she always sent the stamps with the food.

A lady with malice in her heart said, "You don't know whose pocket those stamps end up in!"

Words were spoken that I am sure hurt some of the people present. It would have been nice if this woman had left her tool of malice at home.

The sharp tool of fear is one we do not want in our toolchest of life. I have known people whose health failed because they became afraid of something. They let that fear take away their joy.

A number of times in the Bible, God told his children to "fear not" (Gen. 15:1, 26:24; Isa. 41:10).

Have you ever had a swarm of gnats come around when you were working outside? They were a bother, but you kept on working and fanning them away, and eventually they found a new place to go.

Fears are like that. If we trust in God to help us, and keep moving on, they go away.

A popular toolchest in our part of the country now is the type that fastens behind the cab of a pickup. These toolchests are attractive, they lock, and are easy to take along.

A Christian's toolchest should be just as well qualified. It is easy to always carry a New Testament and is easier yet to take along Scriptures you can quote from memory. They are your tools for winning others.

You do not even have to stop whatever you are doing to use the tool of prayer. I was talking to a person I wanted to win for Christ and as I talked my heart was asking God to give me the right words.

Our chest must have all kinds of small compartments to be filled with Christian virtues.

Once when we were visiting a ranch in southern Texas the rancher proudly showed my husband his new toolchest on his pickup. I paid little attention until he said, "I also bought one for my son's pickup."

That seemed important to me. Who gave me my tools for life? My parents started the collection, my teachers added to those tools, and many I acquired by hard work and experience.

If that rancher felt it was important for him to buy his son a toolchest, it is much more important for us to provide our children with spiritual tools to make their lives more worthwhile.

There is nothing a workman enjoys so much as having the right tool for a task. Examine your life and be sure you possess the right tools for success and happiness. Throw out the tools which only hinder and hurt.

Loving Grace

We're not bettered by complaining,
  Nor by discord which we vent,
And bad spirit needs explaining,
  Which brings on more discontent.

When the day bogs down with worry,
  And the problems multiply;
When the spirit's swamped with hurry,
  And the breath comes with a sigh,

Looking up can give assurance,
  Bring one courage, strength and hope,
Change the prospect, add endurance,
  Lighten loads with which we cope.

It will add much joy to living
  If in confidence we face
Each new day with selfless giving
  Of our best, with loving grace.

J.T. Bolding

13

Life's Green Pastures

He maketh me to lie down in green pastures: he leadeth me beside the still waters.—Ps. 23:2

From the time we are born we seek green pastures. A baby longs for its mother's arms and feels secure at her breasts.

A toddler looks for all kinds of new worlds to conquer and explore.

A six-year-old seeks to be "it" in games at school. When he is chosen to be in the center of the circle he feels a sense of accomplishment.

A teenager feels that his pastures are green when he has a crowd to run with.

Adults are continually looking for greener pastures. They seek to educate their children, to pay the mortgage on their home, then to put up a nest egg for retirement.

Yet God offers us many green pastures that have no connection with material things.

Perhaps the psalmist was worn from cares and battles when he wrote these verses and was trusting his Good Shepherd to lead him to a place of quiet rest and peace.

In Palestine there grows a love and attachment between the

shepherd and his flock. As the sheep rest the shepherd keeps watch. They rest in perfect peace, knowing the shepherd is near.

We also run around seeking greener pastures. But all we really need to do is trust our hearts and lives to the Good Shepherd and let Him lead us into the green pastures of life. We see only the pastures of today, but God sees the whole plan and knows just how and when He will lead us to greener pastures.

Byron makes Bonivard dig footholds in the walls of his dungeon prison. With the aid of the footholds, Bonivard is able to ascend to a window high up on the wall where he is able to see the mountains, sky, and sunshine. He takes courage and learns patience to help him wait.

A young minister wanted a large church to pastor the moment he finished school, but that was not the will of the Father. He needed to work in smaller places, to learn patience and love. When the time came God led him to greener pastures.

In order to enjoy the green pastures human sheep must be willing to follow the leadership of the Shepherd. They must listen to His call and obey His orders. The sheep are not always capable of knowing which pastures really are the greenest, so they must wait for the Shepherd to show the way.

In college Bill offered his heart and hand to a girl he admired. She liked Bill a lot but she knew he was a poor boy. She wanted to marry someone rich, so she spent all her effort and charm on a young man named J.L.

Years later she met Bill at a social function. He had worked hard and was a successful businessman. His wife was dressed in the latest fashion and looked very happy.

Before the evening was over J.L. became so drunk his wife had to take him home. What she thought was a green pasture had turned out to be only a heartache.

It is the will of God for us to have green pastures to rest in where His love and protection make us peaceful and happy.

Many in the world today have the feeling that they are self-sufficient, and thus seek to better themselves without God's help. Yet our heavenly Father delights in giving us our needs.

Earthly parents work hard in order that their children may have the things they need, but much more our Father in heaven longs to give us the best.

We lose the radiance and music of life when we lose our Christian witness. We must tell others of the green pastures and of the Good Shepherd.

Many people follow after leaders of cults because they think they will lead them to green pastures. It is sad that they do not know the one Good Shepherd who can lead them best.

While we were visiting with some friends we said some admiring words about a beautiful house across the street.

"Yes, isn't it beautiful?" our friend said. "But the man who built that house is dead and now his sons and a daughter are fighting in court over the property. He left plenty for each one to be happy and comfortable, but they are jealous over the power in his business. Lawyers will make money and their family love and companionship will wither and die," she said.

Looking at the fine home, I thought with sadness of the widow, as she saw her sons fighting over money and power. Wealth can bring a poverty of soul if we keep looking for more.

A long time ago a novelist made the statement, "Wherever a man lives there will be a thornbush near his door."

Trouble will come to all men from time to time, but for men to be happy, they must have a purpose and a goal. They must conquer the thornbush at their doors, rather than just leaving to search for greener pastures.

In eastern Texas there are cockle burrs that are harmful to the farmers' fields and in western Texas, there are tumbleweeds that blow across hundreds of acres on windy days spreading seed all the way. Each place has its thornbush in the green pasture. Each person has a flaw in their makeup or some other problem, but we must take the time to cope with and conquer those thornbushes as God leads us on to more perfect pastures.

God's Blessings

It's such delight to count the blessings of the Lord;
    To note how always He has been so good to me;
My heart just overflows with gratitude and praise,
    Because His child I have the privilege to be.

He sends the sunshine and the sweet refreshing rain;
    He sends the lovely springtime and the fruitful fall;
The harvest with its rich rewards of golden grain,
    And in His greatness, pours His plenty on us all.

There is no earthly way that we can e'er repay
    What He in grace and love abundantly bestows,
For as, with grateful hearts, we try in vain each day
    To tally up, His blessings ever grow and grow.

J.T. Bolding

14

The Golden Clasp

This is my commandment, That ye love one another, as I have loved you.—John 15:12
Love ye therefore the stranger: for ye were strangers in the land of Egypt.—Deut. 10:19

Love is the golden clasp that holds the world together. Love holds families together when they seem full of discord. Love keeps us working when our tired bodies cry out for rest. Love gives a person a will to live when all seems against him.

A man who survived a concentration camp during World War II, was asked how he stood the suffering and how he lived through it.

"When you have a way to live, you try to find a how," he replied. "I had a wife and baby in America and I knew they were praying for me. Often just the knowledge of their love kept me fighting to live."

Love for others leads to great adventure and to many tears of joy.

> "Love is like a beautiful plant:
>   To grow, it must be fed.
> You have to keep on nourishing it
>   Or someday you'll find it dead."

Author Unknown

Several kinds of love are mentioned in the Bible and all parts of the golden clasp work to keep the world together.

Unselfish Love

Jesus wanted his followers to have unselfish love. He told them, "Thou shalt love they neighbor as thyself."

That is a hard command to follow for Satan tells us to cheat our neighbor and let him get by the best he can on his own.

Almost every year in western Texas we read in the newspapers about a farm tragedy. A farmer may be burned, or injured by machinery. When the neighbors find out, they help him. Long lines of pickups, cotton pickers, trailers, and women bringing food go to that man's farm to gather his crop.

Another example of loving our neighbors is found in the story of a lady working in a department store who was told her husband had incurable cancer. She could not quit her job to stay home with him because there were doctor bills to pay plus trips to a cancer clinic in another town to finance. Their friends helped out by taking up offerings to help meet expenses. We can love our neighbor by seeing his need and trying to help him meet that need. Sometimes we must deny ourselves in order to show love for a neighbor.

Christ gave us the greatest example of unselfish love, when He gave His life for us.

Sincere Love

Romans 12:9 says, "Let love be without dissimulation. Abhor that which is evil; cleave to that which is good."

A young woman I knew went away to teach school. Amid strangers for the first time in her life, she was easy prey for young men. One man vowed his love for her. She knew he often broke dates and made excuses for short-comings, but she married him just the same. Her life was unhappy because she could not tell when he was sincere and when he was just telling her a story to get his way. Eventually their marriage was broken and her explanation was, "He just wasn't sincere."

We see people each Sunday who go to church and say they love Jesus, yet they are not sincere enough in that love to live Christlike lives.

Sincere love is shown when a small child picks a flower and brings it to his mother. The mother accepts that flower as precious and places it in a glass of water.

Impartial Love

Deuteronomy 10:19 says, "Love ye therefore the stranger: for ye were strangers in the land of Egypt."

One spring my husband and I took a trip to the Greek Islands. On the Island of Rhodes we were especially looking for some pretty bells to take to a friend back home. In one shop the clerk was very nice and we found just the bells we wanted. As we were ready to leave he picked up a postcard and handed it to us. "A gift," he said.

It was just a small token, but we were strangers in a strange land and we realized he was kind and wanted us to have a good time.

Think of this verse in another way. Consider the people who are unsaved strangers to us. Are we showing them the kindness we should? Are we as quick to go and help someone in need if they do not belong to our church?

Christ Love

All other loves look pale beside the love Christ had for a lost world. Look at the wonderful privileges we have and think what our country, our lives, and our homes would be if Christ had not come. For the people who do not know Christ, the world is still dark and hopeless. We are the ones to show love to all we meet.

Other types of love mentioned in Scripture are fervent love, abounding love, brotherly love and benevolent love.

Love

A handclasp, our love, always helps to declare;
  A message of comfort may show that we care;
A word to encourage is easy to share;
  They're cups of cold water, in Jesus' dear name.

A smile often lifts a great burden of woe;
  A call may inspire one to get up and go;
A wave may help someone who's feeling so low,
  They're cups of cold water, in Jesus' dear name.

The Lord adds His blessing to what we bestow,
  If humbly it's given, without any show,
In honor of Jesus while through life we go,
  As cups of cold water, in His own dear name.

J.T. Bolding

15

Bridges

Between us and you there is a great gulf fixed. . . .—Luke 16:26
But ye, beloved, building up yourselves on your most holy faith. . . .—Jude 20

Many years ago in eastern Texas two young people were courting. They lived on adjacent farms with a small creek as the boundary line between the farms.

One day when they reached the stage in their courtship where a day could not pass without seeing each other, it rained and rained and the creek filled so high with water that the young man could not cross to see his sweetheart.

He went back to his home, secured an axe, and returned to the creek bank. There he cut down a tall tree and let it fall across the creek. He was then able to cross on the trunk of the fallen tree.

All through life people come to great gulfs and need to build bridges.

Christ came to earth to build the greatest bridge ever known to man. He spanned the gulf between heaven and earth and made a way for us to cross.

In an African village there were two groups of natives who lived on opposite sides of a river. The only way they could communicate was by beating their drums or crossing in a boat.

A stranger came to the bank of the river one day and started to build a bridge. First he put piles deep into the river bottom. Next he put the sills up. Then at last when all was ready, he put a floor on the bridge and rails on the sides to keep people from falling.

We may think of Christ as the piles put down to hold the bridge of our life. If Christ is deep in our hearts, we will have the proper foundation.

We may call the braces and sills, love and unselfishness. We cannot build ourselves up if we do not have these two traits.

Two planks Christ taught us to have in our bridge are prayer and worship that we might draw nearer to Him.

When I was a little girl I often prayed to God. I pictured Him as being close by to destroy all dangers and to keep my loved ones safe.

Many times my father would be away from home for a week at a time holding revival meetings. My mother was afraid at night, but I did not share her fear because God just seemed to be there taking care of us.

Now that I am old, I look back and count the gift of not being afraid as a special blessing given directly to me from God.

We are building a bridge every day between our earthly life and eternity. It is important that that bridge be built of enduring principles, beliefs, and greatest of all, a knowledge of Christ.

If you build your bridges straight, strong, and true, the Great Inspector will look at the bridge you have built and say, "Well done."

> Each day we have the privilege
>   To let the love of God shine through our lives.
> Each day's an opportunity
>   To bring God's hope to those with hopeless eyes.

What if we fail, or just forget
  To pass along God's peace and joy and love?
Some friend may miss the heavenly road
  And never reach the blessed home above.

J.T. Bolding

A small boy built a bridge across a mud puddle for his dog. The dog looked at the mud puddle and just jumped across. No amount of coaxing could get the dog to walk on the makeshift bridge.

There is no way we can bridge the gap from earth to heaven except by the blood of Jesus Christ. Many people attempt to jump across but fall because there is no other way provided than by His blood.

We may think of our church as the bridge where we pass from ignorance to knowledge for there we study to learn the will of God as given to us in the Bible.

A bridge is no good unless it is used. We sometimes drive between our home and Fort Worth, Texas. We pass a place where a fine new bridge has been built, yet just a short way to the side is the old bridge, still intact but unused, because the road to it is blocked.

Only Christ can build a bridge between the sinner and God. If we fail to trust Christ, there is no bridge for us across that great gulf. When we have trusted the bridge and are walking across we should remember the rails on the sides. Those rails may be built of love for Christ as shown by our loyalty, our friendliness to others, and our seeking others to travel with us. Faith and truth will keep us steady in our walk.

One of the sweet bridges Christ built for us was the bridge between now and the hereafter. He said, "I go to prepare a place for you, . . . that where I am, there ye may be also."

A great tragedy happened in the United States a few years ago when a span of a new bridge gave way and several cars plunged into the water many feet below. They trusted a bridge that looked good but was unsafe. There are many things in the world that may look good to us, but the only bridge we can trust is Christ.

Bridges

The long bridges may join the wide shores of a bay,
    Suspended from cables of steel;
And some bridges of concrete join banks of a stream
    For the passage of many a wheel.

There are bridges of words which give passage for thoughts
    Between human minds, it is true,
So that folks understand through exchange of ideas
    How things look from a different view.

But the bridges of thought in the intricate mind
    Of a person who thinks on a plan
Are amazing indeed and a wonderful thing,
    When he reasons as human minds can.

Then the bridges of memory join present and past,
    Bringing back precious hours we have known,
As again we live, through the thoughts of our minds,
    Many things from the days which have flown.

J.T. Bolding

16

Avoiding Realities

I can do all things through Christ which strengtheneth me.—Phil. 4:13
But my God shall supply all your needs according to his riches in glory by Christ Jesus.—Phil. 4:19

We are all tempted at times to avoid realities. If we are shopping and having a good time, we avoid thinking about over-spending. If we are on vacation and are seeing many interesting things, we put off starting for home then drive too fast so we won't be late going back to work.

"Where did the morning go?" I exclaimed one morning when I had been extra busy. We had been out late the night before and slept late. After washing, cleaning a little, and doing seemingly endless chores, the clock said it was noontime.

"Where did the years go?" A man of forty-two exclaimed as he realized his life was half over. He had planned to save money, buy a home, marry a wife, and raise children long before now. What had he been doing?

When he looked at some of his former schoolmates with their families and responsibilities, he felt smug. "What have I got to show for the morning of my life?" he questioned.

Humans often avoid realities until it is too late.

We get wrapped up in making money, establishing ourselves in society, and having a good time. We try to avoid the reality that there is more to life than we are getting out of it.

A man working with a partner in a business trusted his partner completely. When a friend warned him against his partner he laughed. He realized his partner had managed to cheat him out of his share, too late. He avoided the reality.

When noontime comes we can never go back to the morning of life; what we plan to accomplish we must work for now.

We often neglect to serve the Lord to the best of our ability. We think, "Who will feed my family if I take time to go to church?" and "Who will meet my payments if I give to the Lord's work? I will give my time and money when I am older."

Then we wake up one day and realize that the morning of life is gone and we have missed the joys of service. We have missed the blessings given to a faithful servant.

Paul, writing to the church at Philippi, was trying to impress upon them the reality of God. Every Christian could profit from reading the Book of Philippians once a month.

Paul was asking his friends to ask God for what they had need of. He was trying to show them from whom he received his strength and help.

We may try to avoid realities as we face them from time to time, but that does not make them go away. A certain man thought his taxes were too high. First he decided not to pay them. Then he realized he might lose his home if he didn't pay, so he decided to wait until the last day. On the last day his payment was due there happened to be a bad storm, so he could not get to the courthouse. He ended up paying a late penalty for his taxes.

The man was foolish to try to avoid the reality of taxes. We are foolish when we try to avoid the reality that we owe service and loyalty to God. Many a person lets the morning of his life go by, planning to trust Christ at the last moment. That last moment may come on the day of a blizzard and life may be over quickly. Then the penalty for avoiding reality has to be paid for eternity. We must not fail to make a decision about giving our lives to God. This is the most important decision of our life.

Some strangers once invited us to their home for a visit. Some of the attitudes they had and some of the things they did made me say to my husband after we left, "We do not want to get involved with that couple."

In life you will be involved spiritually with one of two forces: God or Satan. Which will you choose?

There is no avoiding the reality that life holds a challenge. What challenge do you seek to meet? We have a life to invest and that life is represented by time, money, talent, and love. Where will we invest our life?

One man was talking to another man about his financial investments. Just to be funny the man said, "I have a fortune invested in my wife's hair."

Yet many people do invest their lives in such things as beauty parlors and nice clothes. Both are good in their place.

I heard a minister say, "Intelligent people will create a worse mess of life than dumb people if they do not have the power of God."

Perhaps he is right, I could not say. The newspapers are sometimes filled with sad stories of rich and successful people fighting in the courts over children or property. Perhaps they never know the joy of trusting as Paul did when he said, "My God shall supply all my needs."

We cannot avoid the reality that only Christians can live without fear. We have the gift of eternal life and salvation. With these we can keep looking up.

Keep Life Simple

Children playing in the sunshine,
  Pleasures simple as you see,
Filling yards with joyous laughter,
  Just as happy as can be,

For they do not need the money
  Some folk feel they have to spend
To enjoy each blissful moment
  And to entertain a friend.

My art teacher says that "simple"
  Is the key word from the start
But it's hard to put in practice
  That good rule in "living" art.

Children are a great deal better
  Than adults are, usually,
But the children spoil so quickly;
  Few grownups live easily.

J.T. Bolding

17

A Wise Bit of Counsel

Commit thy way unto the Lord; trust also in him; and he shall bring it to pass.—Ps. 37:5

As we enter a new year we covet some achievements for our lives.

First of all, most of us want to make some contribution to the good of our fellowman. We long to be able to say, "I helped him when he needed help; or I found a better way for this to be accomplished."

Only by having the desire to help others will we be able to see their needs and offer help. In this new year let us resolve to be aware of others and their needs.

Second, as we come to a new year, we think of all the ways we failed to find peace and contentment in the past. We long for the world to be at peace. We long for our homes to be places of peace and joy.

Third, we want to accomplish something for our Lord and our church. We want to help bring in the kingdom of Christ. We plan to spread the gospel to others both far and near, in a better way.

And last, but by no means least, we want to care more for our loved ones. We want to make those nearest to us happy and contented.

How shall we accomplish these things?

Our Scripture gives us the beginning point: "Commit thy way unto the Lord."

Unless we are committed unto the Lord, how can we be happy and successful? Unless we trust in Him, how can we hope to help others?

First of all, examine your heart and see if you are truly committed to the Lord.

If we commit our money to the bank, we trust that bank to take care of it for us. If we commit our ways and our hearts to the Lord, we must trust that He knows best what we need.

We in our own strength are helpless. Scripture says He is our refuge and strength, a very present help in time of need.

A young guest in our home always hated to eat eggs and drink milk. She felt her mother was too hard on her. Yet when she grew up and became a mother, she made herself eat what she didn't like, to set an example for her children.

It costs something to be a follower. We cannot always have our own desires. We cannot expect the new year to abound with blessings unless we follow the will of our heavenly Father.

We were looking at a concert program that had several pictures of musicians from all over the United States in it.

After the concert we discussed the musicians. We thought of all the years of practice and study they had spent trying to achieve perfection.

The commentator had asked one musician why he wanted to spend his summer in a music school.

The musician replied, "I want the fellowship of other musicians."

As Christians we will grow as we fellowship with other Christians.

Famous musicians do not just join great symphonies full grown. They develop from much practice and self-discipline.

There are many discouraging things in our world today. The

person who commits his way to the Lord has hope for a better world. He has ambition to make his dreams come true. Best of all, he has a loving Father to walk with him each day.

We made many mistakes in the year just passed, we will make some mistakes in the year we are beginning. We do not have to carry our past mistakes on our back forever if we have committed our trust to the One who blots out our mistakes when we ask for His forgiveness. When we are committed, we must look forward, not backward.

We were gathering pretty rocks and shells along a sandy beach. Many people had been there before us and the interesting things were few. We saw one large shell ahead and planned to pick it up last since our sack was getting heavy.

Then before we realized it, a large wave came in and washed out, taking with it the big shell we had planned to get.

If we are not careful the waves of this new year will wash over our plans and take them out to sea.

New Year's Wishes

What shall I wish thee? Treasures
of earth?
Songs in the springtime, pleasure
and mirth?
Flowers on the pathway, skies ever
clear?
Would this insure thee a Happy New
Year?
What shall I wish thee? What can
be found
Bringing thee sunshine all the year
round?
Where is the treasure, lasting and
dear,
That shall insure thee a Happy New
Year?
Faith that increaseth, walking in
light,

Hope that aboundeth happy and bright,
Love that is perfect, casting out fear,
These will insure thee a Happy New
    Year!
Peace in the Savior, rest at His feet,
Smile on His countenance, radiant
    and sweet,
Joy in His presence, Christ ever
    near,
These will insure thee a Happy New
    Year.

Author Unknown

18

The Christmas Journey

Lo, the star, which they saw in the east, went before them, till it came and stood over where the young child was.—Matt. 2:9b

The three men climbed down from their camels and started to ask people questions. They were strangers in the great city of Jerusalem.

"It surprises me there is not a great amount of shouting and joy in the city," one of the weary travelers said.

They stopped in the market place, but no man there had heard of a new King being born.

"Surely someone has heard of the King!" they said. "What a long expensive journey for us to fail. We will go to Herod; perhaps he knows and is keeping the knowledge secret."

All the city was becoming disturbed. Word was spreading quickly over the city of the strange men and their request to see a newborn King.

"Where is He that is born King of the Jews?" Now all the people wondered the question the foreigners had asked.

The men received an audience with Herod. Frankly and honestly they asked, "Where is He that is born King of the Jews?"

Herod was shocked! At great cost of life and money, he had

obtained and held his throne. This imposter must be found and destroyed, he thought.

"Tarry a short while and I will call in my wise men, they will know the answer to your question," the king said.

When all the wisest of the kingdom were assembled before Herod, he asked, "Where will Christ be born?"

The three men sat tired and weary, but determined, waiting and listening.

Throughout their long journey they had felt desert sandstorms, cold nights, fear of robbers, thirst, and hunger. But as long as they kept sight of the star the hardships of the journey did not seem so bad.

Many people then and now are wandering on a trackless desert through life, because they have no star to follow. The star makes the difference in your journey.

In recent years we have seen a generation of youth, a large segment of which seem to have no star in life. We see them from coast to coast, dirty, hungry, and aimless. Somewhere their teachers, pastors, and parents failed to point them to a star.

As the men waited, one of the oldest said that it was written by a prophet long ago that the new King should be born in Bethlehem of Judea.

Herod, consumed with fear and anger, hid it well for he thanked the men for visiting him and said, "When you have found the young child, come back and tell me, so I too may go and worship."

It took more than an earthly power to give the wise men a star to follow. It had to be sent from heaven. They listened to the giver of the star, for directions and went on their way rejoicing.

How blind we are sometimes. We get up in the morning, go about the day's tasks, but don't see or care that others need our help.

People all around the little family in Bethlehem didn't even know of the happenings that took place that night. But shepherds on the quiet hillside heard the Christmas music and wise men far away saw a new star and sought a Lord to worship. How much the others missed.

The wise men came at last to the place where their star stood still and saw a King to worship. Gladly they brought treasures to present to the babe. They saw the glory of God, brought down to earth for the purpose of redemption.

Why did they see the King when others merely passed by?

(1) They were anxious searchers. (2) They sought a King, not just a young child. (3) They saw and worshiped Him.

Think for a moment of the church building where you attend services.

What do you see when you enter for services? What did you enter to see?

If you come to find fault you will find it, for humans are never perfect. But if you come to find fellowship, it also is there.

If you seek light and guidance, you will find it in the teachings of the Word. If you seek power and strength to live better, you will find it by faith in the Holy Spirit.

If you come to worship, the King of kings and Lord of lords will meet you there. Always, there is a star for your journey if you look for it.

Stars In Your Eyes

Where are you going, my fine stalwart friend
    With the clusters of stars in your eyes?
What is your purpose and what, in the end,
    Will you do with your life? Why the sighs?

Stars in your eyes are just fine, so they say
    And they picture great thrills in a boy;
But with a star as a guide for your way,
    You will find a continuing joy.

Purpose and goal as the star for your life
    Give direction and zest for the fray,
And as they guide in the toil and the strife,
    They will dull the temptation to stray.

J.T. Bolding

19

Keep This Lovely Day

And in the morning, then ye shall see the glory of the Lord.—Exod. 16:7a
And he shall be as the light of the morning, when the sun riseth, even a morning without clouds; as the tender grass springing out of the earth by clear shining after rain.—II Sam. 23:4

All children look forward to Christmas Day whether they live where there is much snow and bad weather, or in the South where there is seldom ever a picture postcard Christmas.

Our first Scripture reading isn't necessarily speaking of Christmas, yet how much we long to see the glory of the Lord on Christmas morning.

To children, Christmas is a time for hoping dreams will come true in the way of nice gifts. To parents, it is a time of seeing joy and happiness reflected from the faces of their children. To old people, it is a time of seeing their loved ones together and happy. Christmas is an event, an experience, for old and young alike. Christmas makes us long to do for others. Even the hardest heart is more easily touched at Christmastime.

Christmas is no ordinary day! It is the day when God gave us the greatest gift of all time—the day when One came to earth from all the glories of heaven in order to make a way for us to live in heaven with Him. What lovely thoughts.

Yet there are those who spoil this lovely day by being greedy and selfish.

I am reminded of a family of farm folks with ten children and many grandchildren. The darling son of the family of girls, brought his bride of a few months to the family Christmas party.

The bride, a pretty young woman, had not prepared any gifts for the family. The son had ordered boxes of candy for each of his sisters and a book for each of the brothers-in-law. For the grand-children he had small token gifts. For his mother and his bride he had beautiful lace stoles.

When all the gifts were given out the young bride stormed out saying, "Is this all you bought me?"

"Well, I thought that was enough since I just gave you a diamond for a wedding present," the young man said in embarrassment.

The happy family party was ruined and none of the family tried to make friends with the stranger after her outburst. She had ruined a lovely day with her selfish, ugly words. Never again was she a welcome guest at the family parties.

Many times we spoil Christmas, not by ugly words or deeds, but by simply crowding out the thought of Jesus. We wonder if we have just the right gifts for those we feel obligated to and our thoughts are too jumbled to make room for Christ.

When I was a child, we spent Christmas at my grandparents' home. That was a wonderful time for all the grandchildren. We did not receive any gifts except fruit and stick candy placed in our stockings, while we were asleep. Yet over sixty years later I remember with joy those family times. We often had squirrel dumplings for our Christmas dinner because turkeys were sold or traded for sugar and flour.

We heard the story of Christ's birth told from a small card obtained at the country Sunday school, which met in a public school building. We had time for Christ and we had time to be thankful for our many blessings.

We do not want those hard pioneer days back for our children and grandchildren, but we do want our children to slow down and recognize God's gift to us at Christmastime.

Mary and Joseph were the first to see Jesus in this world. How did they make the day of His birth lovely? They made a warm, safe place for the Him to rest.

New parents dream of and plan what they will give their baby, but love is the greatest gift they can offer.

We seek to make those about us happy because we love them. But at times our love is like that of a little girl I knew.

The little girl helped her neighbor with some house work and the neighbor paid her some money. The child took the money and bought her mother and father a box of candy for Christmas.

When the gifts were opened on Christmas morning the child opened her mother's box of candy and started eating it herself.

We lose sight of the purpose of Christmas when we act selfishly.

There are two things we shouldn't forget about Christmas Day. The first worshipers, the shepherds, went away to be messengers of the good news.

The next worshipers, the wise men, brought gifts.

Telling the story and giving gifts are still the two most important things for worshipers to do.

A young couple with a baby two years old wanted to teach their child about Christmas and its meaning. They told the child about an old couple who lived next door. He was allowed to help put cookies and candy in a box. Then when the box was wrapped, he went with his parents to give the gift to the old folks.

The next year when people started talking of Christmas, the child found a box in his toy chest. He took the box to the kitchen and was emptying the cookie jar into it.

"What are you doing?" the mother asked.

"Taking Christmas next door," he replied.

The child was very young, yet he had learned that the real joy of Christmas was to take a gift of love "next door."

Love

God in His Son came down to earth;
   He brought His love for men,
And now we celebrate His birth
   And sing of it again.

We give our worship and our praise;
   We bow as wise men did;
Our hearts rejoice, our songs we raise,
   Our love must not be hid.

In self forgetfulness we come
   To love our blessed Lord
And pray that we will not, as some,
   Bring sorrow and discord.

Let us, as Jesus Christ above,
   For others seek to bear the yoke
Since love of self is stolen love;
   It's always meant for other folk.

J.T. Bolding

20

The Gospel and the Flag

O Jerusalem, wash thine heart from wickedness, that thou mayest be saved. How long shall thy vain thoughts lodge within thee?—Jer. 4:14

Jeremiah was a great prophet of the Old Testament, but he was unpopular because he wanted the will of God for his country.

The times Jeremiah lived in were very much like our own. There was immorality, wars, cheating, robbing and turning away from God. Jeremiah often seemed to be standing alone against sin and evil.

The people were living in false security. How true that is today. We love our great country, blessed above all others with prosperity and knowledge, yet we are in danger.

We often boast of our self-sufficiency. We feel we can meet any crisis. Yet if we do not wash our hearts from wickedness, will our country be saved?

This is a day of failure as far as nations are concerned. Men in high places have failed to be honest. Democracy has failed. We now have to build private schools for our children to hear the Word of God taught in school. Our teachers are not free to lead a prayer in public classrooms to the One who gave us our great country.

There will be a day of reckoning for America. We could read our Scripture: "O, America, America, wash thine heart from wickedness that thou mayest be saved."

We enjoy singing our national songs, such as the one singer Kate Smith made famous, *God Bless America.*

We love our country—at least most Americans do. Are we going to just stand aside and see the things our grandfathers, husbands, and sons died for, being destroyed?

A Sunday school teacher was trying to talk to her pupils about how good God had been to America.

"Two hundred years! So what!" a teenage boy exclaimed.

The poor teacher was crushed, but told him how other great nations had failed to stand so long.

Patriotism is a matter of the heart, more than the head. Our children must be taught how great our nation has been and will continue to be if we are true patriots.

In our vacation Bible schools we usually use two flags—the Christian flag and the United States flag.

Both flags have meaning to us. When we salute the Christian flag we pay homage to our Lord and Savior. When we salute the United States flag we honor our country and the things for which it stands.

There are three colors in the flag: red, white, and blue.

We may think of red as the blood of Jesus, the blood shed for our salvation. We can seek to help all learn of that blood.

White is for purity. We can start purity at home and seek to be an example for others.

Blue is the background for the stars. It stands for truth. We must start demanding that our nation be run by men who stand for truth and righteousness. The best defense for any nation is its righteousness and humility.

When we look at our flag let it mean peace. Let it stand for brotherhood to all mankind.

Our Land

We thank Thee, Lord, for our good land
   So blest, so great, so very dear,
With opportunity to stand
   And face each day with little fear.

We thank Thee for the fertile plains,
   For valleys clothed in luscious green,
For vast and lovely fields of grain,
   For mountains, lakes, and roads between.

And when Old Glory is unfurled
   To flutter in the breeze above,
Our hearts with freedom's song are thrilled,
   And fill with gratitude and love.

                        J.T. Bolding

21

Thanksgiving

And thou shalt remember all the way which the Lord thy God led thee.—Deut. 8:2a
And from thence, when the brethren heard of us, they came to meet us as far as Appiiforum, and The three taverns: whom when Paul saw, he thanked God, and took courage.—Acts 28:15
It is a good thing to give thanks unto the Lord.—Ps. 92:1

I was in the middle of making a dress when suddenly a thought caused me to stop.

I remembered that I had been very ill, just a year ago, knowing that I might not make it through surgery and if I did, I might have long, hard cobalt or radium treatments.

Now here I was feeling great! Why did I waste the morning sewing when I should have been praising God?

Miracles do still happen. God still listens when people pray. I came through that operation and the doctor said, "I was able to cut out every bit of the malignant parts. You are a lucky girl."

Thanksgiving should be a time of remembering God's wonderful blessings. When we sit down to eat our Thanksgiving dinner we should take time for each member of the family to mention one thing they are thankful for.

In our Scripture reading we see Paul giving thanks and taking courage. Paul had been a prisoner, had suffered shipwreck, and had been threatened with death.

After his long journey, Paul saw kind friends coming to meet him. He was special to someone even if he was a prisoner. He took courage when he saw them and gave thanks to God for bringing him safely that far.

Thanksgiving makes us remember our national history. We think of our forefathers who bravely left their homelands and came to start a free country. We tell stories of the first Thanksgiving Day.

We could go further back than the time of our pilgrim fathers to a time when God led His people out of bondage into freedom. They were slaves in the land of Egypt with no hope of their heavy burdens being lifted, yet God sent a leader to take them out of bondage.

Thanksgiving is a time of remembering the many blessings in our personal lives. Birds sing praises, cats purr with contentment, dogs wag their tails, cows chew their cud. All nature praises God, but why does His greatest creation, man, forget to praise Him?

Paul at one time commanded us, "In every thing give thanks." (I Thess. 5:18).

How could he be so thankful after all the troubles he had?

A friend of ours lost his home in the storm, then before he could take care of the insurance settlement, he was hurt on his job and had to spend time in a hospital.

At first he was inclined to say, "Why did it happen to me?" Then one day his wife came to tell him she had found a house the insurance company would give them a settlement to buy.

He was released from the hospital to go home. He thought the house was just wonderful. Having been good at carpentering he saw many little things he could improve about the place.

"Thank God for letting me keep at least part of my fingers," he told his family. When they moved in, the whole family thanked God for His blessings. They had forgotten to take time to count them before.

In some of his writings Edward W. Bok tells a story of one man's way of showing gratitude and thanksgiving.

Two young men who were in college ran low on funds and had to either raise money or drop out of school. They decided to engage the great Paderewski for a piano recital as they felt there would be enough profit to help them finish school.

The manager for the great pianist wrote and told them that they would have to guarantee a fee of two thousand dollars.

With all confidence, the boys went right on planning the concert. They were sure a large crowd would come. When the concert was over, the total they received was only sixteen hundred dollars. How disappointed they were. The two went to Paderewski and gave him the sixteen hundred dollars plus a note for the other four hundred. They explained how they had been trying to stay in school.

The great man tore up the note and gave them back part of the money.

Years rolled by and the two boys grew rich and famous. War came and Paderewski was striving to keep the people in his homeland of Poland from starving.

Food and supplies began to pour into that stricken country from the United States. Paderewski traveled to Paris to meet the man responsible for the supplies to offer his thanks.

That man was Herbert Hoover. His reply to the thanks of Paderewski was, "That's all right. You don't remember it, but you helped me once when I was a student at college."

When you are discouraged take heart as Paul did, for God knows our problems and only waits for us to ask for His help. We get so buried in our problems that we forget all the times the Lord has led us.

We have much to thank God for. As the psalmist said, "It is a good thing to give thanks unto the Lord."

Thanksgiving

Oh, I thank my dear Lord, whom I'm trying to serve,
That He never does give me just what I deserve.
For if He really did, then I never would get
All the good things in life that I so much enjoy
Like forgiveness of sin, and the songs I employ
Every wonderful day since my Savior I met.

Yes, I thank my dear Lord for His blessings galore;
Though my heart overflows, there seems always some more.
And my gratitude surely shall not ever cease
For the Lord is so good, His salvation to give,
He has promised me that there with Him I shall live
Throughout all of eternity's day in sweet peace.

I'm so thankful to God every day He allows,
That I daily renew unto Him all my vows,
And I try just to walk with my hand in His own
For I really do want His sweet will to be done,
That my life He may use so some child may be won
While His love for each soul I can help to make known.

J.T. Bolding

22

Debts I'll Never Get Paid

This is a faithful saying, and worthy of all acceptation, that Christ Jesus came into the world to save sinners; of whom I am chief.—I Tim. 1:15
Knowing that he which raised up the Lord Jesus shall raise up us also by Jesus, and shall present us with you.—II Cor. 4:14

When my oldest daughter came home from college one weekend I knew she was deeply in love, but I was not prepared for a letter that followed in just a few days.

Her sweetheart had received notice he was being called for military service. He would be allowed to finish the month of school left in that semester. They were going to come home and be married in about three weeks.

My first thought was, "I can't get her ready on such short notice."

But how my friends worked. I never realized what wonderful people they were before. After the wedding was over I felt like I owed favors to half the women in our church.

My daughter's wedding was just as nice as could be. The church was filled with well-wishers and the happy couple never knew for years about all the work that went into that short-notice wedding.

I will never get all those debts of love paid!

But the greatest debt I owe is the one to God's only begotten Son Jesus Christ. Christ opened unto us the gate of everlasting life. Can such a debt be paid?

We are in no way capable of paying the debt of the agony of the cross.

I can picture the women as they arose early and went quietly to the tomb on the first Easter morning. They were carrying spices to anoint a dead body, but found an empty tomb. The risen Lord has no need of spices but He demands your worship and belief.

Luke 24:1-6, gives us the sad picture of the women that morning as they found His body missing, but the verses end on a wonderful note: "He is not here, but is risen" (v.6a).

Easter is a time of choice. The birds in the tree sing because it is their nature to sing. We are above the birds; God gave us the ability to make choices.

We choose each day whether we will serve the one true God, or serve the false gods of the world. What blessings the women would have missed if they had said, "It is too early to get up and besides, we might be in danger."

Christ was their Master and they choose to pay a debt of love by doing what they could.

Every few days we read of someone going bankrupt who chooses not to pay his debts. We feel sad when we read such notices. We think, "There is a person who has given up hope."

When we fail to believe on Christ, we are saying, "We do not choose to pay our debt of love."

Two boys stood before a judge in a Chicago court. The judge gave them a choice of sixty days in jail or probation.

The judge said, "Report to your probation officer and work at being good because for the next crime you commit, I will give you no mercy."

One boy chose to follow as closely as possible the order of the judge. The other boy never reported to his probation officer and was soon in trouble. True to his word, the judge gave him a stiff prison term.

One boy accepted the offer of hope; one rejected it.

The women left the sepulchre with great joy; they had accepted hope.

Easter Morn

They went that first bright Easter morn
    Just at the break of day,
And found the stone that sealed the tomb
    Already rolled away.

As Mary tarried there, the Lord
    Revealed Himself alive,
And since that day through faith in Him,
    With her's, our hopes can thrive.

He is alive; He lives in me;
    My heart's His dwelling place.
My life is new, my hope is sure,
    I'm living by His grace.

J.T. Bolding